MAHATMA GANDHI

Simon Adams

FRANKLIN WATTS
LONDON • SYDNEY

Maps Ian Thompson
Designer Thomas Keenes
Editor Constance Novis
Art Director Jonathan Hair
Editor-in-Chief John C. Miles
Picture Research Susan Mennell

Consultant Eileen Yeo
Professor of Social and Cultural
History, University of Strathclyde

First published in 2002
by Franklin Watts
96 Leonard Street
London
EC2A 4XD

Franklin Watts Australia
56 O'Riordan Street
Alexandria
NSW 2015

ISBN 0 7496 4647 0

Dewey classification: 954.04

A CIP catalogue record
for this book is available
from the British Library.

Printed in Hong Kong/China

Picture credits
Front cover: Topham Picturepoint
(both)
Back cover: Topham Picturepoint
AKG London pp. 5, 7, 20-21, 27, 30,
32-33, 51
Popperfoto pp. 14-15, 43, 44, 52,
56-57, 65, 79, 86-87, 89, 90, 92-93,
94-95, 99 (Reuters/Fabrizi Benusch),
100 (Reuters/Savita Kirloskar)
Topham Picturepoint pp. 2, 3, 9,
10-11, 12, 18, 22-23 ,25, 28-29,
34-35, 38, 41, 46-47, 48-49, 54,
60-61, 62, 66-67, 68, 71, 73, 75, 81,
83, 96-97, 103

JBGAN
1308886

Mahatma Gandhi
1869-1948

Contents

Introduction

To some people a living saint, to others a fraud, Mohandas Karamchand Gandhi influenced people around the world with his philosophy of peace and non-violence.

Mohandas Gandhi was born in western India on 2 October 1869. He was killed in the Indian capital, New Delhi, on 30 January 1948. Apart from two years' training as a lawyer in Britain, he spent the whole of his life first in South Africa and then in India. He was well educated, but shy and physically unimposing. Yet this unassuming man had more impact on the 20th century than almost anyone else. Guiding his homeland – the second most populated country in the world – to independence, he influenced countless millions of people.

In this book, we follow the story of Gandhi from his birth and upbringing in India through his education and family life in Britain and South Africa to the campaigning activities in India that were to dominate his life. Above all, we look at what he taught and how he tried to influence events through his beliefs.

What is remarkable about Gandhi is the way his inquisitive mind picked up ideas from many different religions and philosophies. He moulded these ideas into a belief in non-violent civil resistance – *satyagraha* – that was in direct opposition to the violent methods used by so many other political leaders in the 20th century.

The other notable thing about Gandhi is that he achieved so much, yet he rarely held office in a political party and never became a member of parliament or a government minister. Through the example of his own life and teachings, he directly altered the course of history in India and the world. Some people thought he was a saint. The Indian poet and writer Rabindranath Tagore gave Gandhi the name *Mahatma*, which means "great soul", and the name stayed with him for the rest of his life. Gandhi saw himself as "a politician trying to be a saint".

In a violent and brutal century, Gandhi stands out as one of the most peaceful and remarkable men of his times.

Early life

Mohandas Gandhi was born into a rich and successful family, but the young Mohandas gave no indication that he would become world famous in later life.

Gandhi was born on 2 October 1869 in the tiny, princely state of Porbandar in western India (see map below). At that time, the British ruled India, but many parts of it were still governed by maharajahs (princes) and other local rulers, who controlled affairs in their own territories but pledged their allegiance to Britain. His grandfather Uttamchand Gandhi, father Karamchand and uncle Tulsidas all served as Dewan or Prime Minister to the Prince of Porbandar and other rulers in the region. These appointments gave the Gandhi family respect in the local community and some wealth, and they owned several houses.

The young Mohania

Karamchand Gandhi married four times. His fourth wife, Putlibai, had four children – three sons and a daughter – of whom the youngest was Mohandas Gandhi. As the youngest child, Gandhi was much loved and pampered. His family called him Mohania – a shortened and affectionate version of his real name – and he enjoyed playing games with his toys. At the age of six, he started school in Porbandar and then a year later, changed schools to one in the nearby town of Rajkot, where his family had moved to serve the local prince.

▶ *Gandhi (right), aged 17 in 1886, with his oldest brother Laxmidas, who was a lawyer in Rajkot and later worked for the Porbandar government.*

7

Although, as a child he was surrounded by books, Gandhi was a slow learner and had difficulty with spelling and maths. However, he worked hard and eventually mastered such difficult subjects as geometry and Sanskrit, the ancient language of India. As a teenager, he was smaller than his friends, disliked sports and was very shy. He had also started smoking, and stole money from his family to pay for cigarettes. This was a crime he was later deeply ashamed of.

Early marriage

It is the custom in India for parents to arrange marriages for their children in order to join their two families together. By the time he was seven years old, Gandhi had been engaged three times without his knowledge or consent before, at the age of 13, he was engaged and married to Kasturbai Nakanji, the daughter of a Porbandar merchant. His bride was 13 as well; although they spent a lot of their time apart with their own families, they grew to love each other and their marriage lasted for 62 years. The couple eventually had four sons – Harilal (born in 1887), Manilal (1892), Ramdas (1897) and Devadas (1900). Gandhi

himself believed that children were unready for early marriage, however, and remained opposed to arranged child marriages all his life. Kasturbai could not read or write, and although Gandhi tried to teach her, she never learned. However, she was a clever and determined woman who was Gandhi's equal in many ways.

Life in London

In 1888, at the age of 19, Gandhi left his wife, son Harilal and the rest of his family behind in India and sailed to Britain to study law. He had wanted to study medicine, but a friend of the family suggested that if Gandhi wanted to become a politician like his father, uncle and grandfather, he would need to become a lawyer first. His father had died in 1885, and his mother did not want her youngest son to leave home. In the end she agreed, but as a devout Hindu she made him promise to keep true to his Hindu faith and avoid imitating Englishmen by indulging in temptations such as wine, women and meat!

Gandhi enrolled at the Inner Temple, one of the four inns of court or colleges in London where people study to become lawyers. He was still very shy, but tried to

fit into English society by
taking elocution lessons to
improve his speech, as well
as dance and violin
lessons. He tried to
dress and act like a
stylish English
gentleman:
during the day

*Kasturbai Gandhi in 1915,
33 years after her childhood
marriage to Gandhi. Throughout
her life, she wore a sari in
preference to western clothes.*

he wore dark striped trousers, a striped shirt with a flashy tie and a double-breasted waistcoat, over which he wore a morning coat and top hat. He also carried a silver-topped cane and wore leather shoes and gloves. For the evening, he bought a formal evening suit to wear at dinner and always took great care of his appearance when he went out.

Gandhi also remained faithful to his mother's wishes and did not drink alcohol or eat meat. He was not a rich student, but found that vegetarian food satisfied his hunger. He soon organized a local vegetarian society to learn more about this way of eating, and attended conferences of the National Vegetarian Society and other meetings. He also obeyed his mother's wishes by remaining faithful to Kasturbai, his young wife back home in India.

While in London, he took the opportunity to travel to Europe, visiting France in 1890 to see the huge and impressive Paris Exhibition. He stayed in the city for a week, and went up the newly constructed Eiffel Tower two or

◀ *Gandhi (first row, left) with members of the Vegetarian Society in London in 1890.*

11

As a young law student in London, Gandhi was always smartly dressed.

three times, eating an expensive meal in the restaurant on the first platform, "just for the satisfaction of being able to say that I had my lunch at a great height!" He also studied books on politics and western philosophy, as well as the Bible and other religious works and, for the first time, read the *Bhagavad Gita*, the sacred text of the Hindus. Gandhi himself was a Hindu, but had never read the book before. At first, he read the book in its English translation, but years later he studied it in the original Sanskrit and eventually translated it into his native Gujarati language.

By the time he had passed his final examinations in July 1891 and become a lawyer, Gandhi had educated himself not just in law, but in politics and religion too, exposing himself to ideas from around the world and from different religions to his.

Back home

Gandhi returned to India in the summer of 1891 to discover that his mother had died during his absence. The news had been kept from him because his family knew he was devoted to his mother and did not want him to abandon his law studies in London early to return home to mourn. His son, Harilal, was now four, and his older brothers and sister had children of their own. Gandhi got on well with children, but he was not yet earning enough money to support his own family. His brother, Laxmidas, helped him begin work as a lawyer, but he was a complete failure. During one court case in Bombay Gandhi was so scared and shy that he did not utter even a single word! He also disagreed with the local political agent, or representative of the British government, ruining his chance of following his family into the Prince's government in Porbandar.

At this stage in 1892, Gandhi's career did not look very promising. He had a wife and, by now, two young children to support – his second son Manilal had just been born – but it seemed unlikely he would become a success in India. Luckily, a local Muslim-run business in Porbandar needed a lawyer for one year to represent their interests in southern Africa, and offered the job to Gandhi. He accepted eagerly, and in April 1893 he left his wife and family behind and sailed across the Indian Ocean to start a new life in a new continent.

Campaigning in southern Africa

In 1893 Gandhi went to southern Africa on a one-year contract. He stayed for 21 years, during which time he became known as a campaigner for Indian civil rights.

Today South Africa is a united, multi-racial country. In the 1890s it consisted of four states: the two British-controlled territories of Cape Colony and Natal and the two Afrikaans-speaking Boer states of Transvaal (also called the South African Republic) and the Orange Free State. All four states were dominated by white settlers. The native Black people and the small Indian population, which numbered about 75,000 out of a total of about six million, had very few rights.

Indentured labour

In 1845, the British began to grow tea, coffee and sugar cane in Natal. However the local Black population did not want to work on land they considered was theirs. The British therefore began to import workers from India on five-year contracts, or indentures, to labour on the farms.

▼ *Many Indians worked as indentured labourers on the sugar plantations of Natal. The work was backbreaking and hard and the pay was low.*

Indentured labourers

The Indians had come to southern Africa from their homeland to work as indentured labour, that is on fixed-term contracts, in the sugar plantations and later, in the mines. Some had stayed on after their contracts had finished, and were joined by "free Indians", who came from India to work for themselves as traders and in other professions. All Indians suffered from racial harassment, and were subject to daily curfews and other restrictions on their liberty.

Confronting racism

Gandhi met this racism as soon as he arrived in the country, when he was forbidden to wear his turban in court. Turbans were worn by both Hindus and Muslims, but only Muslims were allowed to wear them in the white-run courts. When he travelled from Durban in Natal, where he had landed, inland to Pretoria in the Transvaal, in order to argue his first case for his employers, he was forced to move out of his first-class compartment into third-class, even though he had a first-class ticket. Indians were forbidden by the railway company to travel first class in order not to offend the white passengers. He also failed to get a room in a hotel because he was not white, and was forced to accept lodgings in a house.

Fighting for rights

This experience convinced Gandhi that the Indian community must organize itself to fight for its basic rights in southern Africa. He arranged a meeting of Indian merchants in Pretoria and spoke to them in public. This occasion

◀ Southern Africa at the time Gandhi lived there. Transvaal, where Johannesburg is located, was also called the South African Republic.

was to be the first time he had ever made a political speech. Gandhi urged them to learn English, so that they could fit into society more easily, and to be cleaner and dress more smartly. The link between personal self-improvement and political and social struggle was a common theme in every one of Gandhi's campaigns throughout his life.

In 1894 Gandhi prepared to sail home, as the legal case was now settled. He was persuaded to stay, however, by Muslim traders in Natal, who feared that the government was about to take away many of their rights. The next year he helped to launch the Natal Indian Congress, which took up a number of important issues that concerned the Indian community. Among these were the right to vote as free people and the charges indentured Indians had to pay to buy their freedom. Although Congress did not always win what it was campaigning for, it had considerable success in organizing the Indian people of southern Africa.

Staying on

By now, Gandhi had become the leading Indian politician in the four states. He took up many cases for indentured

labourers and championed their cause with governments and in the courts. He addressed conferences, wrote pamphlets and letters to newspapers, circulated petitions and did all he could to raise the issue of Indian rights. He did not argue for full Indian equality, because he recognized that the small white community felt threatened by the much larger Black and Indian community around it. Rather, he argued for equality before the law. This meant that Indians would receive just treatment, not prejudice. Since Indians were subjects of the British Empire, he said that they should have the same equality under its laws as every other British subject, white, Black or Indian.

By 1896, Gandhi had been in southern Africa for three years and was missing his family. He realized, however, that he could not abandon his political and legal work for the Indian community and so he decided to remain. He therefore took six months' leave and returned home to India to collect his wife and children. While there, he made a number of

Kasturbai and her four sons in South Africa, 1902: Manilal (far left), Devadas, Ramdas (seated) and Harilal, the eldest.

speeches about conditions in southern Africa. These speeches were reported in southern African newspapers, angering many white people. When Gandhi returned to southern Africa in December 1896, he was greeted by a hostile crowd when his ship docked at Durban. His friends advised him to stay on board ship, but he ignored them and disembarked in broad daylight. The crowd attacked him, and he only managed to escape with his life when the wife of the Durban Police Commissioner – who happened to be passing by – intervened and saved him. Gandhi refused to pursue criminal charges against his attackers, arguing that it was better to forgive them than punish them.

Indian Ambulance Corps

In 1899, the Boer War broke out in southern Africa between the British and the two Boer states of Transvaal and the Orange Free State. Gandhi argued that since Indians wanted to become full and equal subjects of the British Empire, they must also accept its obligations and fight for the Empire when asked. However, Gandhi himself did not believe in violence, so he organized the Indian

Ambulance Corps to help the wounded. More than 300 free and 800 indentured Indians – Hindus, Muslims and Christians – joined the Corps, which saved the lives of many British soldiers until it was disbanded in 1900. To honour their contribution to the war effort, the British gave Gandhi and others its official War Medal.

While in southern Africa, Gandhi began to consider how best to live his life. He did not like luxuries such as good food or fine clothing, but was unsure what he really did believe in. In 1904, he took a train journey from Johannesburg in the Transvaal to Durban. A friend gave him a book to read: *Unto This Last: Four Essays on the First Principles of Political Economy* by John Ruskin. Ruskin was a British writer and critic whose subjects ranged from art and culture to economics and politics. In this book, Ruskin argued that people should seek "not greater wealth but simpler pleasure, not higher fortune but deeper felicity [happiness]", and that it was worth living a life of labour.

◀ *Gandhi (circled) surrounded by members of the Indian Ambulance Corps during the Boer War in southern Africa in 1899.*

The Phoenix Settlement

Gandhi was very affected by Ruskin's message and translated it into action by buying some land outside Durban. There he created an *ashram*, or spiritual community, known as the Phoenix Settlement. Here people of any race, colour or creed could live a simple life together. All that was asked of them was that they obey the rules of the ashram. These included honesty, celibacy, non-violence, fearlessness, *swadesh* – wearing only simple clothes with no jewellery – and giving up all personal possessions except those required to feed and clothe oneself. All residents, including children, participated in the day-to-day running of the ashram and everyone undertook some physical labour each day. For his part Gandhi took a vow of *brahmacharya*, or celibacy, since he already had four children and now wanted to control his personal desires and live a more ascetic life in order to devote his energies fully to his public work. His wife, Kasturbai, did not object, and Gandhi remained celibate for the rest of his life.

▶ *Settlers at the Phoenix Settlement pose for a photograph in 1906. Gandhi (circled) is standing in the third row, third from left.*

Satyagraha

In southern Africa, Gandhi developed a new tactic to use in his campaign for Indian rights. He called it *satyagraha*, which means non-violent civil resistance.

The Boer War in southern Africa ended in 1902 with the defeat of the two independent Boer states by the British. Gandhi hoped that the newly united South Africa would grant political rights to its Indian population in return for the support they had given to the British during the war. However, the main concern of the British was to improve relationships with the Boers. The rights of Indians and Blacks were ignored.

The struggle begins

In 1903, Gandhi opened a law practice in Johannesburg, the main city of the Transvaal. He represented many Indians in legal cases against the government and soon became the leading Indian politician both here and in the rest of the country. The Transvaal provincial government had established an Asiatic Department to deal with Indians, and made it plain that they would never get political rights in the province.

In 1906, the Transvaal government proposed that all Indian men, women and children over eight had to register with the authorities, get finger-printed and receive a certificate which they had to carry with them at all times. Any Indian who failed to register faced a fine or imprisonment – or could even be deported from the Transvaal. This proposal reduced Indians to second-class citizens and, if extended elsewhere in the country, threatened their very existence in southern Africa. It also threatened Indian women in particular, since it would allow a police officer to interrogate a woman on the street or enter her home uninvited. This was deeply offensive to many Indians, both Muslim and Hindu, because traditionally, Indian women lived private lives away from the public eye, and did not speak to people in the street.

▶ *Gandhi with some of his legal colleagues in front of his office in Johannesburg in 1905. The office was kept busy representing the Indian community.*

Satyagraha

Gandhi responded to this proposal by calling a meeting of the Indian population at the Imperial Theatre in Johannesburg on 11 September 1906. Almost 3,000 Indians attended – men and women, Hindus and Muslims, rich and poor, "free" Indians and indentured labourers – and agreed not to comply with the proposed legislation if it became law. This was a brave step that could lead to an appearance in court and possible imprisonment and other hardships.

A campaign of non-violent or passive resistance of this sort had no name, so Gandhi offered a prize for anyone coming up with something suitable. His cousin Maganlal suggested *sadagraha*, which means "firmness in a good cause", but

Satyagraha

Gandhi saw satyagraha as a positive act of civil resistance, a term he preferred to civil disobedience. Not just a passive act of non-compliance with the law, satyagraha required positive, active participation in any campaign. "It is," he said, "the vindication of truth not by infliction of suffering on the opponent but on one's self." Violence therefore was not met with more violence, but with peace and strength of mind.

Gandhi himself changed this to satyagraha: "*satya*" means truth or love, "*agraha*" means firmness or force. Satyagraha therefore means truth-force, or love-force.

The Black Act

The Asian Registration Act – or the Black Act, as the Indians called it, because it classed them along with the Black population – came into force on 31 July 1907. Some Indians obeyed it, but most did not, among them Gandhi, who was arrested and charged on 11 January 1908. He was found guilty of disobeying the Act and sentenced to two months in jail.

At this point, General Jan Smuts, once a leading Boer general against the British, but now a leading member of the Transvaal government, offered a compromise: if the Indians would register voluntarily, the Act would be repealed. Gandhi agreed to this and was the first to register when he was freed from prison. But the government failed to carry out its agreement. Gandhi was physically attacked by his former supporters for betraying them. He therefore renewed the campaign with greater vigour, urging thousands of Indians to burn their registration certificates in August 1908. Many were arrested and went to prison as a result.

Gandhi then decided to widen the campaign. The Black Act had the effect of denying Indians the right to immigrate and settle in the Transvaal without valid registration documents. Individual Indians volunteered to test this ban by entering the Transvaal illegally from neighbouring Natal, risking arrest if they were caught, which many thousands were. Gandhi himself was arrested and imprisoned in the Transvaal in 1908 and again in 1909 for not having a registration card. At one point, 2,500 Indians

▶ By the time this photograph was taken of General Smuts in 1931, he had become a leading politician in the British Empire.

out of a total of 13,000 Indians in the Transvaal were in prison and 6,000 had fled the province. However the government refused to back down and the campaign continued.

Tolstoy Farm

Gandhi read widely and corresponded regularly with writers and thinkers all over the world. He particularly liked the teachings of Leo Tolstoy, the Russian author of *War and Peace*, who had abandoned his wealth and now lived a simple life in the countryside of Russia. In 1910, a friend of Gandhi's bought a 445-hectare piece of land 33 km outside Johannesburg and gave it to him as a refuge for satyagrahis (those involved in satyagraha campaigns) and for their families to use during their lengthy

campaigns against the government. Gandhi named it Tolstoy Farm and used it to develop his ideas about communal living. He moved there with his family and soon became an excellent baker, grinding his own wheat to produce enough bread to feed the inhabitants. He also made caramel coffee to replace the tea and coffee they refused to drink, because both drinks are stimulants, like alcohol, and made sandals and clothes for them to wear.

At first, the population of the farm consisted of 40 young men, three old men, five women, and about 30 children, of whom five were girls. Hindus, Muslims, Christians, vegetarians and meat-eaters mixed well together. They all contributed to the work of the farm, sowing and reaping the wheat harvest, collecting fruit from the large orchard and water from the wells, and constructing new farm buildings. Some of the men made furniture, such as tables and benches, but there were no chairs or beds, and everyone slept under blankets on the ground outside, unless it was raining.

◀ *Members of Tolstoy Farm in 1914. Most of the men are wearing western clothes, although the women are wearing traditional Indian saris.*

The new union

In 1910, South Africa became a united, independent nation within the British Empire, but Indians gained no new rights in this new country. The government promised to repeal the Black Act but not its restriction on Indian immigration between provinces. It also refused to abolish the annual "poll tax" of three pounds on each Indian who had bought his freedom from indentured labour. In addition, in March 1913, the Supreme Court ruled that only Christian marriages were legal in South Africa, which made Hindu and Muslim marriages invalid.

Faced with these three attacks, the campaign of satyagraha gained in strength. Many women joined in, including Kasturbai, Gandhi's wife. A group of "Natal sisters", as Gandhi called them, were arrested when they entered the Transvaal illegally. Many more Indian women then joined the campaign and they too were arrested. Indian miners in the Natal coalfields went on strike. In its attempt to crack down on the strike, the police arrested thousands of miners, two

◀ *During the satyagraha campaign in 1913, Gandhi abandoned European clothes and appeared in public shaven-headed.*

of whom were killed and many injured. Several thousand more went to prison, including Gandhi. In protest against the government's action, he stopped wearing western clothes. His campaign and imprisonment attracted worldwide attention, and the government grew increasingly embarrassed by the publicity.

Victory

On 30 June 1914, Gandhi and his old adversary, General Jan Smuts, reached agreement. The government agreed to end the poll tax on indentured labourers, stop all indentured labour by 1920, recognize Hindu and Muslim marriages and give Indians limited rights of movement between provinces if they carried an identity card. Although this compromise did not give everything the Indians had demanded, it did recognize their basic rights and gave them some status in South Africa.

By now Gandhi had been away from India for 21 years and was homesick for his country. He realized, too, that he had achieved all he could for the Indian community in South Africa and so, on 18 July 1914, he left Africa for the last time to return home.

The British in India

The British had ruled India for more than 100 years by the time Gandhi was born in 1869. It became his lifetime's work to achieve independence for his homeland.

The first people known to have lived in India created the civilization of the Indus Valley in the west of the country, which flourished about 2500 BC. Since then, the country had been invaded 26 times. Each one of those invaders – from the Aryans in 1500 BC to the Moguls in the 1500s – arrived from the north across the Hindu Kush mountains into the plains of north-west India. The exception were the British, the last invaders, who came by sea.

The Europeans arrive

The British were the latest in a series of maritime arrivals from Europe, but they were the only ones to invade and occupy the subcontinent. In 1497, the Portuguese navigator Vasco da Gama had found a sea route from Europe round the southern tip of Africa across the Indian Ocean to India. Portuguese, Dutch and then French traders made the same voyage, seeking opportunities to buy and sell goods with local rulers and merchants along the lengthy Indian coastline. The Europeans established trading posts in suitable harbours and anchorages and developed a thriving trade in textiles, rare hardwoods, gemstones and other items.

The British soon followed their European neighbours and rivals in the form of the East India Company.

▼ *Proclamation of Queen Victoria as Empress of India on New Year's Day 1877 in Delhi, in the presence of the Prince of Wales, who is in the pavilion on the left.*

The East India Company

During the late 1500s, the Dutch gained full control of the rich spice trade from the islands of the Far East to Europe. British merchants wanted to gain a share of this lucrative trade. In 1600, therefore, Queen Elizabeth I of England granted a group of London merchants a charter which gave them a monopoly on all trade between Asia and England. The East India Company originally intended to compete with the Dutch in the Far East, but it soon focused on building up trade with India.

At first, the company set up trading posts along the coast in Bombay, Calcutta and Madras and established good relations with the Indian Mogul emperor. Successful wars against Portugal, Holland, and France led to a vast increase in the company's power and influence in India, with its European rivals eventually restricted to a few small trading posts along the coast.

During the 18th century, however, the East India Company gradually changed its emphasis from trade to conquest. It formed military alliances with maharajahs and other local rulers friendly to the company, but attacked those it opposed and took over their lands.

◀ *During the Indian Mutiny of 1857–1858, the governor's residence at Lucknow was besieged by rebellious Indian army units. This photograph shows the result.*

In 1757 Colonel Robert Clive, an agent of the East India Company, defeated the Mogul Governor of Bengal at the Battle of Plassey. As a result, the Company acquired a large part of eastern India, and in 1774 appointed Warren Hastings to be the first Governor-General of India. The Company's power continued to increase, so that when, in 1818, it crushed the Maratha Empire in southern India, the last challenge to the Company's rule in India had disappeared.

The mutiny

In May 1857, a widespread mutiny broke out in India against East India Company rule. Over the years, the Company had imposed taxes on farmers, confiscated lands and replaced Indian customs and practices with British ones. Resentment against the Company built up until Indian sepoys (Indian soldiers serving the East India Company) mutinied in protest at having to handle gun cartridges that had been greased with either pig or cow fat, which offended the religious beliefs of Muslims and Hindus respectively. The mutiny started in the northern city of Meerut and soon spread to Delhi and across the rest of the country. The mutiny

was put down with considerable force by the Company's soldiers, but it spelt the end of the East India Company's control over the country.

The Raj

In 1858 the East India Company was abolished by the British parliament and the British government took control of India in what was known as the British Raj, or rule. For the next 89 years, India was a British colony ruled by a viceroy or governor. Local maharajahs and other rulers retained considerable power over their own lands and were in theory independent of Britain. In reality they had to pledge allegiance to the British crown and were advised by local agents of the British government in India. Other parts of the country were governed directly by the British.

In 1876, Queen Victoria of Britain took the title Empress of India, although she never set foot in the country. The British built roads, railways and telegraph systems, constructed bridges and irrigation systems, and set up a huge civil service to govern the vast country.

▶ *This map from the early 1900s shows the extent of British India.*

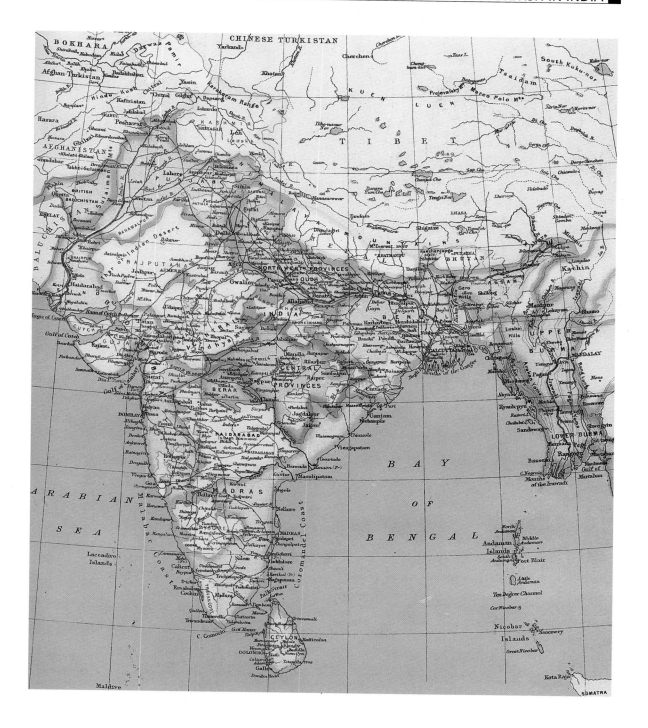

By 1886, the British Raj ruled what are now five countries: India, Pakistan, Bangladesh, Sri Lanka and Burma, as well as various islands and other coastal lands around the Indian Ocean. India was by far the wealthiest and most populous part of the British Empire, and was known as the "jewel in the crown". Indian cotton fed the huge textile mills of Lancashire and its tea watered the mouths of the British. However, the British did little to build up Indian industry, preferring to

export its raw materials to Britain, to be manufactured there, and then returned as finished goods for Indians to buy. In this way, Britain gained both huge wealth and employment from its Indian empire, while leaving Indian industry relatively underdeveloped, with few resources and little new machinery.

Opposition to the British

Although the British were relatively efficient and moderate in their rule over India, they were still foreigners who had invaded and conquered the country and considered the native Indians to be a subject race. Indians had limited power over their own local affairs and had no role in central government. The Raj was administered by a huge civil service, but despite British promises to employ and promote more Indians, by 1915, Indians held only one in twenty positions in the service, and all of these were at a low level. By 1923, the position had improved slightly, so that Indians held one in ten posts, but as before, British civil servants dominated the administration.

◀ *Under the Raj, railways were laid throughout India and every sizeable town and city had its own railway station.*

The British also used the tactic of divide and rule to keep Indians divided among themselves. At times, Hindus were favoured over Muslims, and then vice versa; and native Indian rulers ran parts of the country while the British ran the rest. In this way, the British kept the Indian people disunited and ensured that they always had some local rulers who were willing to support them.

Political reform

In 1885, the Indian National Congress was established by the viceroy, Lord Dufferin, as an annual forum for educated Indians to discuss political and constitutional reform in co operation with the British. Its first presidents and secretaries were all British politicians or civil servants, but by the 1920s the Indian National Congress had changed to become the leading political party of India. A strong central organization was established and branches set up in every province and district. A mass membership supported the party. The Congress Party now became the main vehicle for Gandhi's campaigns.

Back in India

When Gandhi returned to India in 1915, he still believed in the fairness of the British and their empire. A decade later, he was making plans to remove them from India for good.

Gandhi returned to India on 9 January 1915, famous for his activities in South Africa. Many expected him to take an active role in Indian politics, but he had been away for 22 years and had little experience of life in his homeland. A close friend, Gopal Krishna Gokhale, president of the influential Servants of India Society, advised him to travel around India for a year with "his ears open but his mouth shut" and keep out of national politics. He took this advice, and soon came face to face with the poverty and backwardness of village life, which he had never experienced before. He realized that he must first address local social concerns, rather than tackle the bigger issue of how India was to be governed just yet.

The untouchables

In May 1915, Gandhi and his family settled across the River Sabarmati from the textile-making city of Ahmedabad, in Gujarat, western India. There he established the Satyagraha Ashram, where his friends and growing numbers of

▶ *Mohandas Gandhi and his wife Kasturbai on their return to India from South Africa in 1915. At this stage, Gandhi was little known in his native country.*

The caste system

Hindus believed that everyone was born into a caste or social class they could not leave. *Brahmans*, or priests, formed the top caste, *kshatriyas*, or rulers and soldiers, formed the second, *vaisyas*, or traders and farmers, formed the third, and *sudras*, the workers, the fourth. Gandhi belonged to the vaisya caste. Beneath these four castes were the untouchables, the lowest caste of all, whose role in life was to perform the most menial tasks, such as cleaning. Higher-caste Hindus believed that they could be polluted if they met an untouchable, so untouchables were forced to live apart form the rest of society. As a result, they were among the poorest and least well educated people in India.

followers could live and work together. The number of residents varied from 30 to 230; they planted and harvested food, spun and wove cloth and studied together. The Ashram was funded by the wealthy textile owners of Ahmedabad and the shipping owners of Bombay. Gandhi, however, upset his funders, and many others, when he welcomed a family of untouchables into the ashram. Gandhi believed that untouchables had just the same rights as everyone else, and should be treated with equal dignity. He called them *harijans*, or "children of god", and continued to treat them with respect throughout his life.

Mahatma

On his tour of India, Gandhi met the poet and writer Rabindranath Tagore. Tagore had won the Nobel Prize for literature in 1913, the first Indian to win this important prize. He had done much to introduce Indian literature and ideas to the western world and admired Gandhi enormously. He saw that Gandhi possessed a spiritual quality lacking in most people and started to call him *Mahatma*, or "great soul". The name stayed with Gandhi for the rest of his life.

The indigo farmers

By 1917, Gandhi had travelled widely across India and was now ready to enter national politics. He responded to a plea for help from a peasant farmer from Champaran, in Bihar Province, north-east India. Farmers in the region were forced to set aside part of their own land to plant indigo – used to dye cloth – for their British landlords. All the profits from the crop had to be given to the landlords. The farmers resented this imposition and were ready to fight and even go to prison to get rid of this unfair system.

Gandhi visited the region and learned the facts for himself. His survey led to a government inquiry into the plight of the indigo farmers. Gandhi demanded that the farmers be allowed to keep half of their indigo profits, while the commission recommended only a quarter. Gandhi accepted the compromise; although he had not won everything the farmers wanted, he had exposed British exploitation of Indian farmers and helped them improve their working conditions.

▶ *Many untouchables lived in poverty and had few belongings of their own. The untouchable family shown here live in a squalid shack.*

▲ *From 1915 Gandhi travelled widely around India. He hoped that by entering politics he could improve the lives of peasants such as this man from Bombay.*

Amritsar

Gandhi's partial success in Champaran encouraged him to adopt the tactics of satyagraha he had developed in South Africa. The opportunity came in 1919, when the British government proposed to introduce the Rowlatt Bills, named after a committee of enquiry into Indian justice headed by a British judge, Sir Sidney Rowlatt. He and his committee recommended that the restrictions on civil liberty and the press censorship put in place during World War One (1914–18) continue in peacetime. In addition, known troublemakers were to be held in preventative detention and the right of appeal against certain crimes withdrawn. In 1917 the British government had promised to give India self-government within the British Empire. Gandhi believed that the Rowlatt reforms went against that pledge and were both oppressive and unfair.

On 30 March 1919, Gandhi therefore proposed in Delhi that a *hartal* be called. A "hartal" is an ancient Indian form of popular protest or strike, involving prayers, fasting and processions. The hartal was a great success, as Hindus and Muslims across India united behind

Gandhi. Shops closed, workers stopped work, children did not go to school and India ground to a halt.

However, the hartal caused outbreaks of violence across the country. The government responded by attacking and arresting demonstrators. In the north-western city of Amritsar, in the Punjab, Brigadier-General Dyer responded to the deaths of three Europeans by prohibiting processions and meetings. However, 20,000 unarmed strikers assembled at Jallianwalla Bagh, a rectangular piece of waste ground surrounded by walls, on 13 April. Dyer sent troops to stop the meeting and, without issuing any warning, ordered them to open fire: 379 Indians were killed and 1,137 wounded before the troops ceased fire.

The Amritsar Massacre, as it became known, was a turning point in British rule in India. Trust between the British and their Indian subjects broke down, and the campaign against British rule grew much more fierce. Gandhi was shocked by the violence, and immediately called off the hartal. He believed he had made a "Himalayan miscalculation" by encouraging masses of people to participate in a satyagraha for which they were untrained and lacked the necessary discipline and self-control. The campaign, however, had been a success, because the British government did not enact the Rowlatt Bills.

Entering politics

In April 1920, Gandhi took a decisive step into national politics when he became President of the All-India Home Rule League. He urged a policy of non-co-operation with the British, a policy adopted by the Congress Party later in the year. Congress also approved Gandhi's proposal that it campaign for swaraj, or home rule, within the British Empire if possible, or outside if not. By now, Gandhi was the undisputed, unofficial leader of India. Thousands of Hindus and Muslims followed his call to boycott British rule, refusing to serve in the courts and returning British honours and awards. Many more left their government jobs while others burned imported textiles and foreign-made clothes and started to wear their own homespun cloth.

Gandhi extended his anti-British campaign when he called for a new satyagraha of non-payment of taxes in

▼ *The aftermath of the Amritsar Massacre, 1919. Workers construct gallows to hang Indian troublemakers.*

Bardoli, Gujarat, to start on 8 February 1922. The idea was to cripple the administration slowly, by spreading the campaign from district to district across India. However, violence broke out before the campaign started and 22 village policemen were killed when their police station was attacked by a local mob. Once again, Gandhi was appalled

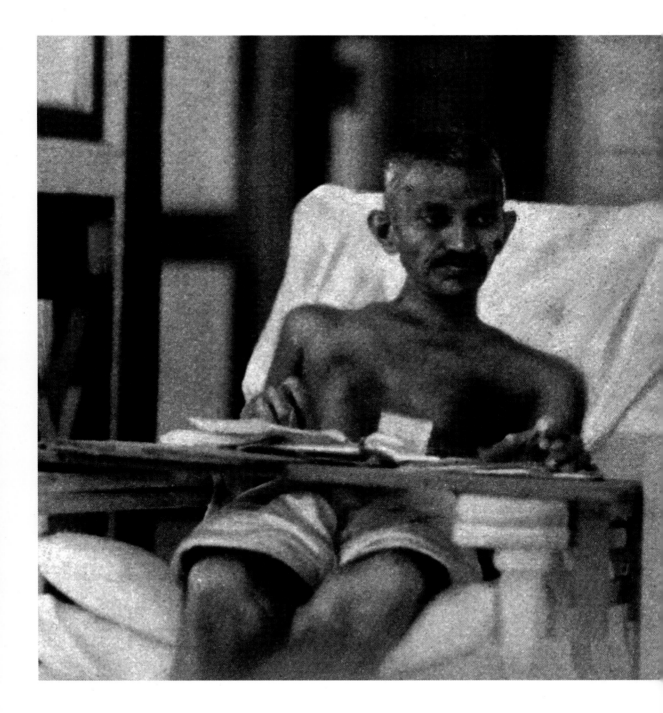

by the violence and called the satyagraha off. The British seized on his weakness and on 10 March 1922 arrested him for inciting civil unrest. The court in Ahmedabad found Gandhi guilty of sedition (undermining the authority of the state) and, on 18 March, sentenced him to six years' imprisonment.

While in prison, Gandhi read, studied and began to write his autobiography. In his absence, the non-co-operation movement fell apart and violence broke out between Hindus and Muslims. When he was eventually released from prison in September 1924 as a result of acute appendicitis, he began a 21-day fast to bring the two sides together. His action had some effect, but Gandhi decided that he should withdraw from active politics and concentrate on his social campaigns. In 1925 he served as President of the Congress Party for that year, but in December he ended his presidency with the announcement that he would have a year of "political silence" at his ashram at Ahmedabad in order to rest and renew his body and soul.

After his release from prison in 1924 due to ill health, Gandhi convalesced at the seaside, where he wrote to his friends and read many books.

Personal beliefs

Gandhi's beliefs were deeply held, and influenced every aspect of his personal and political life.

Gandhi saw all aspects of human life as a single unity, that is that the mind, body and spirit are connected with each other and cannot be separated. He believed, therefore, that what a person thought, what they ate, how well they were, how they behaved and what they did every day, should all be linked. In order to change one of these aspects of life, one had to look at them all. Only then when the entire body was in balance could one attempt to influence or change another person. In other words, reform yourself, before you attempt to reform anyone else. In all his campaigns, Gandhi always practised what he preached, only recommending a course of action if he was already doing it or was prepared to undertake it himself.

Religious beliefs

Gandhi was born a Hindu but was very tolerant of other religions and believed that all of them contained truths that should be appreciated by everybody, regardless of their own religion. He read and studied both the Christian Bible and the Muslim Koran, as well as the religious books of other faiths, and held them all in great respect.

Gandhi was particularly inspired by Jainism, an Indian religion founded in about 500 BC. Jains believe in non-violence towards all living things in everyday life and many devout Jains take vows of *brahmacharya* (abstinence from sexual activity) and *satya* (to tell the truth). Gandhi practised all three of these things during his adult life. Because he accepted all religions, he worked hard to unite them in co-operation and friendship. In India, this proved difficult, as Hindus and Muslims often fought each other. He quoted the old Indian saying that "India must see through both the Hindu eye and the Muslim eye otherwise she is partly blind," but his message of love and unity was often drowned out by hatred and violence.

▶ *Throughout his life, Gandhi was a great writer, keeping up a vast correspondence with friends and admirers around the world.*

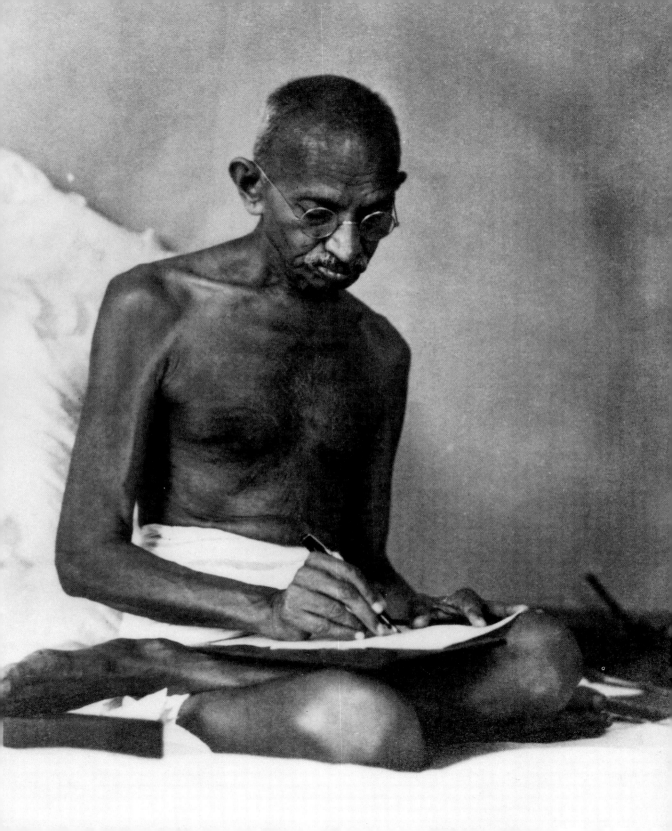

Gandhi was not afraid of new ideas, and was not afraid to challenge his own Hindu beliefs, as his lifelong campaign on behalf of the untouchables and his opposition to child marriages both show. He was also not afraid to change his mind. At first he held the Hindu belief that marriages between different castes and different religions were wrong, but he later changed his mind and encouraged such mixed marriages in order to bring the different castes and religions together.

Gandhi opened his mind to new ideas by reading a wide range of religious, philosophical and political books. He wrote a stream of newspaper articles, pamphlets and books, as well as editing weekly newspapers in South Africa and later India. He regularly received about a hundred letters a day and personally replied to many of them by hand; to others he dictated replies or instructed his secretaries how to respond. Through his vast correspondence, Gandhi remained in touch with many thousands of friends and supporters in India and around the world, and used them to keep up with the latest

◀ *Hindu high priests conducted ceremonies to purify untouchables, but nonetheless, untouchables were rarely allowed to enter temples in their own right.*

thinking and to spread his own ideas worldwide.

Diet and fasting

When Gandhi went to London in 1888 to study law, he kept his mother's promise to remain a vegetarian. From then on, he was careful about what he ate, and lived mainly on a diet of fresh and sun-dried fruits, nuts, seeds and goats' milk. He refused to drink cows' milk because of the cruel way cows were milked, and would not eat eggs. By the time he came back to India in 1915, he had made a vow never to eat more than five items of food a day, and never to eat after sunset.

Gandhi regularly fasted to purify his mind and body and concentrate his

Fasting

Throughout his life, Gandhi undertook fasts, that is, not eating food for a few hours or days. He believed that fasts purified his mind and body and allowed him to concentrate his thoughts on more important issues. At first, his fasts were purely personal acts, but after 1913 he fasted 17 times as a political act in order to achieve non-violent change. Gandhi was probably the first public figure to use fasts as a tool to achieve political aims.

thoughts. In 1913 he fasted to protest against the treatment of Indians in South Africa, the first of the 17 political fasts he undertook, five of them in prison. As he became more famous, these fasts attracted international attention, especially when in 1947 and 1948 he announced that he would fast to death in order to prevent Hindu–Muslim violence.

▶ *Gandhi believed that spinning was both a useful occupation and a political statement.*

Spinning

At the start of his adult life, Gandhi wore the formal suits and ties of a western lawyer. In December 1913, he appeared in public wearing a knee-length white smock, an extended loincloth round his legs and sandals: he explained that he had abandoned western clothing to mourn those Indians who had died in the satyagraha protests that year. By 1921, he had simplified his dress even more, wearing just a simple white cotton loincloth and sandals, and shaving his head. When it was cold, he wrapped himself up in a *khaddar*, or sheet. It is this image of a small, slim, middle-aged Gandhi wearing the clothes of a simple peasant that is famous around the world.

Gandhi's simple clothes reflected his belief that India must turn away from imported western ideas and become self-sufficient and confident in itself. India produced a vast amount of raw cotton, but this was exported to Britain to be turned into clothes and finished textiles before it was exported back to India again for sale.

Gandhi promoted the idea of *swardeshi*, the use of home-grown and home-spun cloth (*khadi*) and home manufactured goods only, and wanted Indians to spin their own cotton and make their own clothes as a political statement against British rule and domination of their country. He encouraged Indians to burn their western clothes as a protest against British rule and urged them to spin and weave for at least one hour a day in order to revive the life and economy of their town or village and to restore personal and national esteem. "Any single district," he wrote,

Saint or politician?

During his lifetime, many people were unsure whether Gandhi was a politician or a holy man. When he lived in South Africa from 1893 to 1914, he observed that "Men say I am a saint losing myself in politics. The fact is that I am a politician trying my hardest to be a saint." In later life, he saw no distinction between the two, and used his religious beliefs for the good of everyone.

"that can be fully organized for khaddar [the spinning of khadi] is, if it is also trained for suffering, ready for civil disobedience." Khadi thus led to self-rule. As a symbol of this, in 1921 he designed a flag for the Congress Party with a Buddhist *chakra*, or spinning wheel, on it. The chakra forms the centrepiece of the flag of independent India today.

For Gandhi, "nothing in the political world is more important than the spinning wheel." To set an example, he therefore only wore clothes he had spun from native cotton himself, and expected his followers to do the same. As he spun for a few hours each day, he used the time to think and consider his future actions and to turn his mind "Godward", as he said.

The Salt March

In 1930 Gandhi and his supporters walked 368 km to the seashore. It was the most important walk in the history of modern India.

During his silent year of 1926, Gandhi rarely left his ashram and spent hours at his spinning wheel. By now, Gandhi was a respected politician throughout India and many millions of people had heard him speak or had read his many leaflets and newspaper articles. His campaigns on behalf of the indigo farmers and the untouchables, and his leadership of the hartal in opposition to the Rowlatt Bills had brought him immense prestige and many Indians believed that he would lead them peacefully towards independence. However, Gandhi was now in his late 50s and a growing number of Indians felt that his non-violent, gradual approach to ending

▶ *On 12 March 1930, Gandhi and 78 volunteers set out from Ahmedabad to walk 368 km to the coast, where they planned the symbolic manufacture of salt from the sea in defiance of British laws.*

British rule was not producing results quickly enough. Within a year, however, Gandhi had seized the initiative and dominated Indian politics once again.

Return to Bardoli

In November 1927, the British viceroy, Lord Irwin, asked Gandhi and other Indian leaders to come to the capital, Delhi. There he announced that a British government commission of enquiry, headed by Sir John Simon, a leading British politician, was to visit India to examine its government and make proposals for political reform. However, no Indians would serve on the commission nor would they be consulted about its activities.

Members of the Congress Party and other Indian political groups immediately refused to have anything to do with the commission. When the commission arrived in Bombay in February 1928, it was greeted with black flags and chanting demonstrators shouting "Go home, Simon!" Gandhi took the opportunity to revive his satyagraha tax strike in Bardoli, which he had called off six years earlier after the massacre of the 22 village policemen. About 87,000 peasants in Bardoli refused to pay a 22 per cent tax increase. As a result British tax collectors seized their possessions, including their carts and their valuable milk-giving water buffalo, and sold them in lieu of tax. Later the government threatened to seize whole farms and sell them off. This time the peasants' protest was entirely peaceful, despite the large number of arrests and police brutality against the protestors. Help flowed in from the rest of India, and in August the government gave way, cancelled the tax increase, and returned all confiscated land and possessions to their owners. Gandhi and the people of Bardoli had shown that satyagraha could work and win results.

The Salt March

By the end of 1928, Gandhi had lost all faith in the British Empire and was firmly in favour of an independent government for India. He therefore issued a warning that if dominion status – that is independence within the British Empire – had not been granted within one year, by 31 December 1929, then he would lead a massive campaign to force the British out. The viceroy attempted to reach a compromise in December 1929,

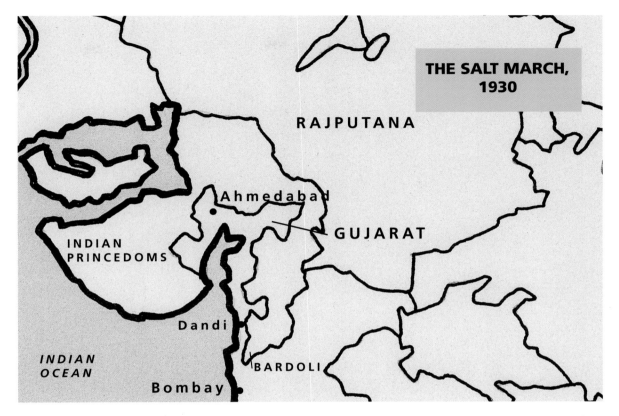

THE SALT MARCH, 1930

RAJPUTANA

Ahmedabad

GUJARAT

INDIAN
PRINCEDOMS

Dandi

INDIAN
OCEAN

BARDOLI

Bombay

but refused to begin discussions on Indian independence. The Congress Party then responded by stating that its aim was full independence for India, either within or outside the British Empire, and promised a campaign of satyagraha to include non-payment of taxes and other acts of civil disobedience.

The form of satyagraha chosen by Gandhi was unusual and not at all obvious. On 12 March 1930, he set out from his ashram outside Ahmedabad with 78 volunteers and headed south towards the Indian Ocean at Dandi, just north of Bardoli, 368 km away. There he proposed to pick up salt from the seashore. Under the Salt Act of 1882, the British government had the total monopoly on the manufacture and sale of salt. Gandhi proposed to break this law by making his own salt from the sea. By seizing on this minor but symbolic injustice of British rule, Gandhi hoped to attract huge publicity so that the effect of this

this satyagraha would ripple out across the country.

Many Indians attacked the Salt March as unnecessary or irrelevant, but Gandhi's slow march towards the sea – he covered about 20 kilometres a day and arrived at Dandi on 5 April – soon attracted enormous crowds, who sprinkled water on the road and put down green branches for Gandhi to walk on. Peasants knelt at the side of the road as the marchers passed and many prayed for its success. Several times each day, the march halted, and large crowds gathered to hear Gandhi give a speech urging them to wear khadi, keep clean and healthy, stop child marriages, and, when the time came, break the salt laws.

In the early morning of 6 April 1930, Gandhi went for a ceremonial bath in the sea and then came ashore to pick up a fragment of salt. In this simple way, Gandhi broke the law: the effect of this single act was enormous. Within a week, much of India erupted in non-violent protest. Millions began to make their own salt and burn imported British cloth,

◄ *Gandhi and other Indian leaders attended a round-table conference in London in autumn 1931 to discuss the future government of India.*

hartals were launched, and other protests organized. Many women joined the protests for the first time. Although Gandhi was arrested on 4 May, his followers continued the peaceful protest, although some were killed when 2,500 protestors tried to occupy a local salt works. This event attracted worldwide coverage, helping to spread the message of the Salt March around the world.

By the end of 1930, Gandhi, other Congress leaders, and about 100,000 demonstrators were in prison. The viceroy, Lord Irwin, was forced to act. On 26 January 1931 he released Gandhi and the other leaders from prison. After lengthy discussions, the two men agreed a pact: the production of salt for personal use by people living in coastal areas would be allowed, all demonstrators in prison would be released, and Gandhi was to represent the Congress Party at a great conference in London to discuss the constitution.

In return, Gandhi called off the satyagraha. He had not won everything he had wanted, but the sheer size and

◀ *Gandhi received a warm welcome from workers when he visited their textile mills at Darwen, Lancashire in September 1931.*

peaceful nature of the protest had proved beyond doubt that a well-targeted satyagraha was an effective tool towards ending British rule in India.

Talks in London

Gandhi arrived in London on 12 September 1931 and stayed until 5 December. He lived in the East End of London and walked the eight kilometres to the centre where the talks were held, every day. He took tea with King George V and Queen Mary at Buckingham Palace, home of the royal family, met the film actor Charlie Chaplin, and talked with groups of students and workers.

Gandhi even went to Lancashire, where raw Indian cotton was turned into finished clothes for export to India. Gandhi's campaign in favour of khadi would have created a huge loss of jobs for the Lancashire textile workers, but here, as elsewhere, Gandhi was given a warm welcome. He charmed everyone with his friendliness and wit, and received enormous and favourable coverage in the newspapers. The exception was Winston Churchill, a member of the British parliament (and future prime minister) and a leading member of the previous

Conservative government which had recently lost office. The Conservatives supported increased home rule, although not independence, for India, a policy Churchill strongly opposed. He described Gandhi as a "half-naked fakir" and refused to meet him.

Back to prison

The round-table conference was a failure. Gandhi wanted to discuss independence, but other Indian leaders were more concerned about the rights of their own religious groups, while the British had no intention of letting go of India. After visits to France and Switzerland, Gandhi returned to India at the end of December 1931 and within two weeks he was imprisoned by the new viceroy, Lord Willingdon.

While he was in prison, the British government announced that it was preparing a new constitution with separate electorates for Hindus and untouchables. That meant they would vote separately for their own representatives, not all together as Indians. Gandhi was strongly opposed to this plan, which went against his belief that untouchables should be welcomed as

Hindus, not shunned. On 13 September 1932, he announced that, on 20 September, he would start a "perpetual fast unto death from food of any kind save water" in protest. At 11.30 a.m. on that day, he took a final meal of lemon juice and honey with hot water and began his fast at noon. Millions joined him in his fast for the day and sang prayers on his behalf.

Gandhi was now almost 63 and his fast caused his health to deteriorate quickly. Politicians in India and Britain rushed to find an agreement that would end his fast. A compromise – the Yervada Pact, named after the prison in Poona where Gandhi was kept – was worked out on 26 September. The untouchables were reserved a number of seats in the new parliament, so Gandhi agreed to end his fast. As the compromise was being discussed, millions of Hindus across the country agreed to admit untouchables into their temples, bringing them into the Hindu community for the first time ever. Gandhi had won a huge advance for his beloved harijans.

▶ *Policemen guarded Gandhi during his stay in London, but here in London's East End, as elsewhere in the country, his reception was friendly.*

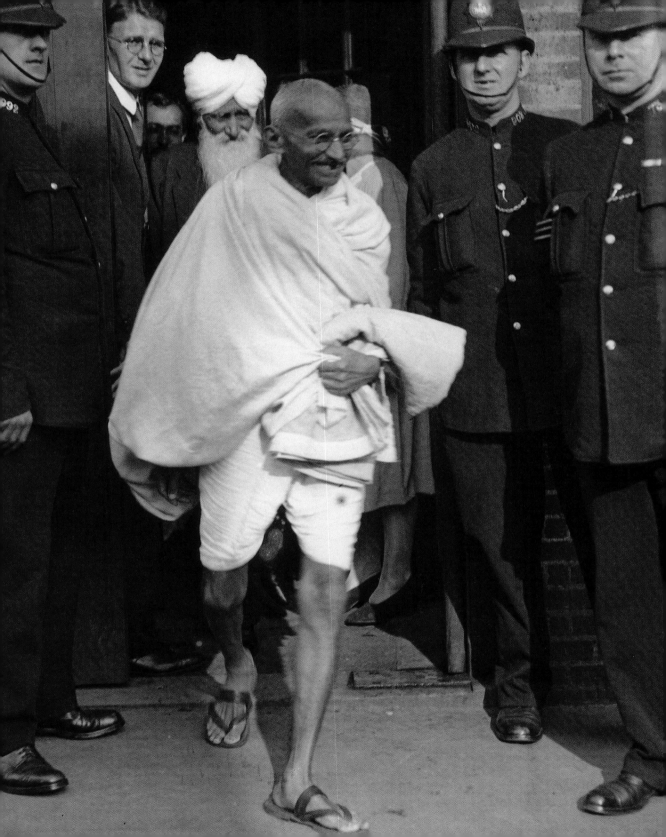

"Quit India"

During much of the 1930s, Gandhi withdrew from active politics. India, meanwhile, moved closer towards independence from Britain.

After the success of his fast in September 1932, Gandhi was released from prison on 8 May 1933. Once again he decided to step back from politics and devote his life to social causes, particularly welfare work for harijans and other poor people. He later wrote that, "I have always held that a parliamentary programme at all times is the least of a nation's activity. The most important and permanent work is done outside." He therefore went on a 20,000-km tour of India to help the harijans, stopping in villages to see how they were treated.

In some places, he was shocked to find militant Hindus adopting his own tactics of non-violent protest against him by preventing him entering temples because of his support for the untouchables and his belief in Hindu-Muslim unity. Elsewhere they waved black flags in protest against him and shouted him down at his meetings.

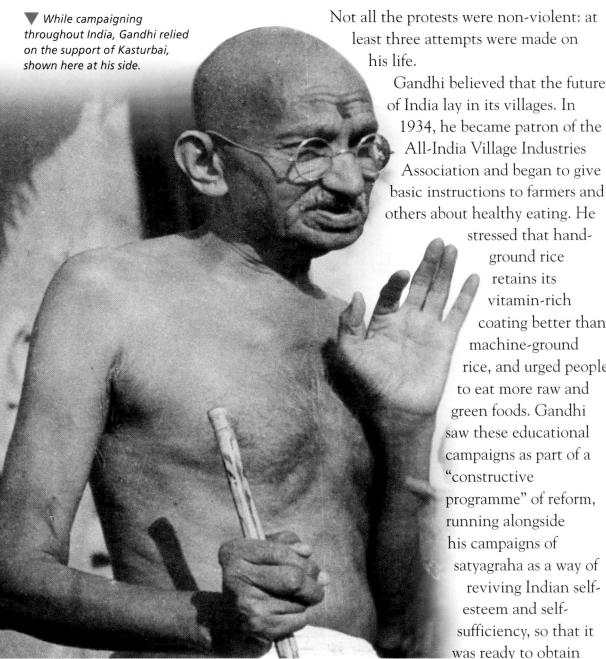

▼ *While campaigning throughout India, Gandhi relied on the support of Kasturbai, shown here at his side.*

Not all the protests were non-violent: at least three attempts were made on his life.

Gandhi believed that the future of India lay in its villages. In 1934, he became patron of the All-India Village Industries Association and began to give basic instructions to farmers and others about healthy eating. He stressed that hand-ground rice retains its vitamin-rich coating better than machine-ground rice, and urged people to eat more raw and green foods. Gandhi saw these educational campaigns as part of a "constructive programme" of reform, running alongside his campaigns of satyagraha as a way of reviving Indian self-esteem and self-sufficiency, so that it was ready to obtain independence from Britain and govern itself as a modern nation.

Gandhi based many of his campaigns of this period at the Sevagram ("village service") Ashram in Wardha, central India, which he established in 1933. He gave his previous ashram at Ahmedabad to harijans and used his new ashram as a type of social laboratory, where he could try out his reforming experiments. Many of his main supporters at the ashram were women, whom Gandhi regarded as equal in status to men. He believed that any laws or customs that deprived women of equality should be ended and he therefore campaigned for the end to the ban on

child widows remarrying and other Hindu customs and practices that discriminated against women.

A halfway step

In 1935 the British parliament passed the Government of India Act, which gave the country a new constitution. It gave self-government to eleven British provinces, which were to join the princely states that made up the rest of India, in a federal structure. Although this move towards federation never took place, the new constitution did allow both women and untouchables the right to vote, increasing the size of the Indian electorate in the eleven self-governing provinces from six and a half million to 35 million. In the elections held in 1937–8 for the various new governments, the Congress Party won 70 per cent of the vote, establishing it firmly as the main political party of India.

Not every Indian supported the Congress Party, however. Many Muslims felt threatened by the changes, which they saw as leading to a Hindu-dominated India. One such person was

◀ Gandhi conducts a prayer meeting at the Sevagram Ashram at Wardha in the 1930s.

Muhammad Ali Jinnah, who left the Congress Party in 1934 to organize the Muslim League. Other Muslim members of Congress followed him in 1935 and the League campaigned against Congress in the 1937–8 elections. Relations between the two political parties became very strained when the Congress Party refused to share power with the Muslim League in the new governments of mixed Hindu–Muslim provinces.

The world at war

In September 1939 World War Two broke out in Europe, after Nazi Germany, led by Adolf Hitler, invaded Poland. Britain and France came to Poland's aid and declared war against Germany. As part of the British Empire, India found itself at war, and Indian troops fought alongside the British, as they had in World War One twenty-five years earlier.

The outbreak of war put Congress in a difficult situation. On the one hand it campaigned hard against the British to achieve independence, but on the other hand it did not want to see Britain lose the war against Germany. However, Britain had declared war on behalf of India without consulting any Indian leaders. The Congress Party therefore asked Britain to announce that it would give India independence after the war, in return for which it would support the British as an equal partner and ally during the war. When the viceroy refused, Congress asked Gandhi to lead a campaign of satyagraha against Britain.

Gandhi was a pacifist but, as in World War One, he supported the British. However, the British had imposed tough wartime restrictions on individual freedom, which angered many Indians. Gandhi decided that the best tactic was therefore to focus on one issue – the official ban on propaganda against the war – since he would not lead any campaign that exploited British weaknesses within the war situation. He chose a novel form of protest: a person-by-person satyagraha. One by one, Gandhi nominated a single well-known satyagrahi – including prominent members of the Congress Party – to challenge the restriction and thereby face arrest. The publicity about each case soon mounted as more than 23,000 satyagrahis went to prison.

For some Indians, this campaign did not go far enough. One militantly nationalist group within Congress, led by Subhas Chandra Bose, argued that now was the time to destroy British rule by force, since the British would be unable to spare enough troops to put down the revolt. This split in the ranks of Congress helped the Muslim League. The League took the British side and also began to argue for a separate and independent Muslim state for those parts of India where the majority of the population were Muslims, leaving the rest of India to consist of the Hindu-dominated parts of the country.

"Quit India"

In December 1941 Japan attacked the US fleet at Pearl Harbor in the Pacific Ocean, bringing the United States into the war against Japan, Germany and Italy and also into the alliance with Britain and France. Japanese armies began to sweep down through South-East Asia towards India. The British government feared that Japan might invade India, helped by Indian nationalists, such as

▶ *In August 1942 Gandhi attended the conference in Bombay where the Congress Party launched its Quit India campaign. The next day, Gandhi was arrested and imprisoned by the British.*

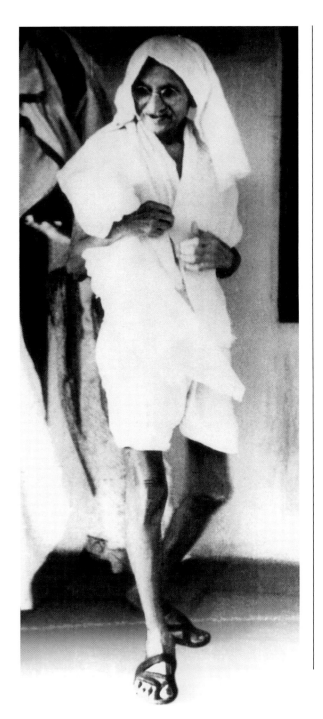

some of those within the Congress Party aggressively campaigning for Indian independence. The British government therefore decided to send a mission to India headed by Sir Stafford Cripps, a Labour Member of Parliament and former ambassador to the USSR. Cripps arrived in March 1942, with a series of proposals designed to obtain Indian co-operation with the British during the war. He proposed that after the war Britain set up an independent Indian Union which each province and princely state could decide whether to join. This meant that a princely state or a province dominated by the Muslim League could decide not to join a union dominated by Hindus and the Congress Party. This proposal fell well short of the Congress Party's demand for an independent, united India.

Gandhi met Cripps in Delhi on 27 March 1942, and was shown the as yet unpublished proposals. "After a brief study," recalled Gandhi later, "I said to Cripps, 'Why did you come if this is what you have to offer? If this is your entire proposal to India, I would advise you to take the next plane home.' 'I will consider that,' Cripps replied." Discussions between Cripps and the

Congress Party continued until 9 April, when Congress finally rejected the Cripps proposals. Later, the Muslim League and the political parties representing Sikhs and harijans all rejected the plan as well. Cripps left India on 12 April 1942 without an agreement.

In response to Cripps' failure, the Congress Party met in Bombay on 8 August 1942 and passed a resolution demanding that Britain "quit India" now or face civil disobedience. A day later, Gandhi and other Congress leaders were arrested and sent to prison for anti-British activities. Riots, violence, and acts of sabotage broke out across India in protest. Police stations and government buildings were set alight, railway lines were ripped up, telegraph poles and wires pulled down, and some British officials were attacked; a few were killed. In parts of the country, Indians set up their own village and town governments and ignored the British altogether. Although these attempts at self-government were largely for propaganda, effective British rule was not fully restored until 1944. In response to these events, the British Prime Minister, Winston Churchill, who was no supporter of Gandhi or Indian independence, declared that he had "not become the King's first minister in order to preside over the liquidation of the British Empire." Independence looked as far away as ever.

Death of Kasturbai

Gandhi was kept in prison for almost two years, the last time he was to be imprisoned. In total, he had spent 2,089 days in Indian and 249 days in South African prisons – more than six years. While in prison, he undertook a 21-day hunger strike. On 6 May 1944, he was eventually released owing to a severe attack of malaria.

His release was overshadowed, however, by the death of his wife Kasturbai on 22 February that year. She had gone to jail with him in 1942 and died in his arms in prison. They had been married for 62 years and she was Gandhi's constant companion and support. Gandhi was devastated by her death: "I cannot imagine life without Ba [his nickname for her] … Her passing has left a vacuum never to be filled."

▶ *Gandhi was devastated at the death of his wife, Kasturbai. "I am going now," she said to him. "We have known many joys and sorrows."*

Two Indias?

During the early 1940s, religious tension between Hindus and Muslims threatened to tear India apart. Gandhi was determined to keep India united.

After the death of Kasturbai and his subsequent release from prison in May 1944, Gandhi retreated to a villa on the seashore at Juhu Beach, near Bombay, provided by a wealthy friend. There he mourned for his wife and recovered his strength after his severe bout of malaria in prison. He did not rush to renew his campaign against the British, as two and a half million Indians were fighting for the British against the Japanese and Germans and he was sure that he would be rearrested if he did anything that might harm the war effort.

Gandhi versus Jinnah

By autumn 1944, Gandhi was ready to re-enter politics. The political situation in India was changing fast, as many Muslims now wanted to divide India along religious lines, with one state for Muslims and one for Hindus. Gandhi, however, firmly believed in a united, secular (that is, non-religious) India. His main opponent was Muhammad Ali Jinnah, leader of the Muslim League, who wanted to create the Muslim state of Pakistan, consisting of Muslim-dominated provinces in the east and west of India.

Jinnah was seven years younger than Gandhi and born in the same part of India as him. His family were originally Hindus who had converted to Islam, but Jinnah was not a devout Muslim: he drank alcohol, ate pork (both of which were forbidden to Muslims), and rarely visited a mosque. He also married a non-Muslim woman, while his only daughter married a Christian. Jinnah had once been a member of the Congress Party but left in 1934 to organize the Muslim League as a rival, campaigning organization. He was a proud man, and resented the popularity of Gandhi and the other Congress leaders. In every way he was the opposite of Gandhi, for while

▶ *Gandhi at the villa near Bombay in 1944. He would regularly appear at the fence surrounding the property to hold prayer meetings.*

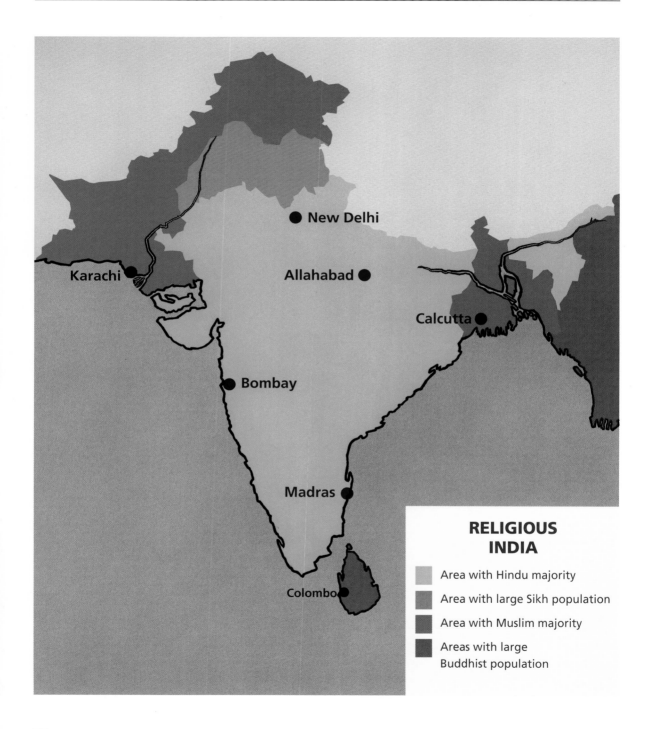

RELIGIOUS INDIA

- Area with Hindu majority
- Area with large Sikh population
- Area with Muslim majority
- Areas with large Buddhist population

the irreligious Jinnah wanted a religious Muslim state of Pakistan, the religious Gandhi wanted to keep united the secular state of India.

The problem of partition

The two men met in September 1944 for talks about the possible partition of India into two states. Three provinces in the far west – Sind, the North-west Frontier Province, and Baluchistan – had huge Muslim majorities, but three other provinces – the Punjab in the west and Bengal and Assam in the east – were more evenly divided between Muslims and Hindus. Jinnah wanted all six to be included in Pakistan, while Gandhi suggested that those parts of the three divided states where Muslims were in a majority join the other three provinces in Pakistan if they wished. In addition, Jinnah wanted the British to divide India before independence, while Gandhi wanted to create an independent India first, from which the Muslim states could later leave if they wished.

The gap between Jinnah and Gandhi was so great that the talks collapsed without agreement. As a result, Jinnah increased his own prestige at the expense of Gandhi, and weakened Gandhi's claim that Congress spoke for all Indians, not just Hindus.

The beginning of the end

In June 1945, as the war against Japan drew to a close, the viceroy, Lord Wavell, released from prison those Congress leaders who had been in jail since 1942. He then summoned India's politicians – Hindu and Muslim – to talks at the summer capital of Simla (the main Indian capital was now New Delhi, but it was too hot in the summer, so the British moved the government up into the mountains in the north). Gandhi attended the conference, but only as a private citizen, as he did not want to repeat the failure of his talks with Jinnah.

Wavell proposed to set up an executive council representing all the different religions and political parties to govern India and prepare it for eventual independence. Jinnah, however, refused to nominate any Muslim representatives, and the conference collapsed.

Meanwhile, a general election in Britain held in July 1945 led to the defeat of Prime Minister Winston Churchill, a strong opponent of Indian independence, and his Conservative Party and a landslide victory for the Labour Party, led by Clement Attlee, which supported India's independence. The new government immediately announced that it sought "an early realization of self-government in India" and called for elections across India. The viceroy would then convene an assembly of those representatives successful at the election to draft a new constitution for an independent, united India. Prisoners were released, and those 7,000 or so Indian nationalists led by Subhas Chandra Bose who had formed an army to fight for independence from Britain by supporting the Japanese were pardoned.

In March 1946, the British government sent a delegation to India consisting of Sir Stafford Cripps, who had led the previous mission in 1942, Lord Pethick-Lawrence, Secretary of State for India, and A. V. Alexander, First Lord of the Admiralty, all three of whom knew Gandhi well. By this time, the new leader of Congress was Pandit ("wise man") Nehru, a long-term associate of Gandhi, who had spent nine years in British prisons since 1921. Nehru was far more practical than Gandhi, and better able to negotiate with both Jinnah and the British. Gandhi continued to play a role in the background, keeping the peace between the different groups in Congress.

The British mission decided that it was impracticable to partition India, since many Hindus would be included in the six provinces of Pakistan, while many Muslims would live in Hindu-dominated provinces in India. It also decided that to divide the three provinces of Bengal, Punjab, and Assam along religious lines would be unfair to both sides. In particular, it would cause huge difficulties in the Punjab, which was the homeland of the Sikhs, who were neither Hindu nor Muslim. It therefore proposed to create a unified, federal India consisting of the British provinces and the native states, governed by a federal government dealing with foreign affairs, defence, and communications. In the federal parliament, a majority of those voting, and a majority of both Hindus and Muslims, would be required to decide any major religious or communal issue.

▶ *Gandhi and Nehru were old friends, but very different in personality and beliefs. Most importantly, Nehru was not religious and was therefore more acceptable to Muslims than many Congress leaders.*

Both Congress and the Muslim League decided, reluctantly, to accept the plan, but when the viceroy refused to allow Jinnah to veto the inclusion of a Muslim in the list of Congress Party candidates for office in the transitional government – because he wanted to claim all Muslim support for himself – Jinnah and the Muslim League withdrew from the agreement. On 12 August 1946, the viceroy therefore asked Pandit Nehru to form a government. Nehru asked Jinnah to join, but he refused.

Hindus and Muslims

Hinduism is the ancient religion of the Indian people. It has no founder and no single creed but has evolved from many different traditions and beliefs over 3,000 years. Hindus worship many gods, although most believe in an impersonal "Absolute", called Brahma, the creator.

Islam began with the prophet Muhammad, who was born in Mecca, Arabia, in about 571. He preached that there is only one God, Allah, whose words are written in the Koran. Islam spread to nothern India in the early eighth century.

Hindus and Muslims have often lived peacefully together but both fear domination by the other. Sometimes this leads to violence between the two communities.

Violent breakdown

In response to the formation of the new government and Muslim League exclusion from it, Jinnah declared 16 August Direct Action Day. Four days of rioting broke out in Calcutta, in the east of India, with at least 5,000 killed and 15,000 wounded. The riots spread across India, leading to many deaths. Gandhi's belief in non-violence was ignored.

Some of the worst outrages occurred in October in the Noakhali district of East Bengal, where Muslims murdered Hindus, and then in Bihar, where Hindus reacted by murdering Muslims. Nehru went to Bihar to restrain the Hindus while Gandhi proposed to "fast unto death" to stop the violence. Other Congress leaders begged him not to do this, however. On 6 November, Gandhi therefore travelled to Bengal to urge reconciliation. By the time he left in March 1947, he had visited 49 villages in Noakhali. He held prayer meetings, and tried to get Hindus and Muslims to live together. Gandhi was now 77, but his strength of purpose helped him survive this tiring pilgrimage.

▶ *From November 1946 to March 1947, Gandhi travelled round the villages of East Bengal, trying to bring peace to the divided Noakhali district.*

Partition and independence

India finally achieved independence from Britain in August 1947. For Gandhi, the event was no cause for celebration.

On 20 February 1947, Clement Attlee, the British Prime Minister, announced in the House of Commons that Britain would leave India "by a date not later than June 1948". Lord Louis Mountbatten, a member of the British royal family and Supreme Allied Commander for South-East Asia in World War Two, was named as the 20th, and last, viceroy of India.

The arrival of Mountbatten

Mountbatten arrived in India on 22 March and immediately held separate meetings with Gandhi, Jinnah and other leaders in order to get to know them as people, so that he could form his own views about the future of India and its independence from British rule. Mountbatten soon realized that the timetable he had been given by Attlee was too long, for the violence in Bihar and Bengal was followed by Muslim massacres of Sikhs in the Punjab and an uprising in the North-West Frontier Province. This violence threatened to overwhelm the entire country unless a decision about partition was made soon. Mountbatten later recalled: "I arrived out there [India] to find this terrible pendulum of massacres swinging wider and wider; if it was not stopped there was no telling where India might end."

However, Congress wanted to maintain an undivided India and would only accept patition as a last resort in order to avoid civil war. But it refused to let large numbers of Hindus living in Bengal, Assam and Punjab become part of a separate Muslim state of Pakistan. Jinnah and the Muslim League wanted the partition of India, but would not accept any further partition of these three provinces.

▼ Muhammad Ali Jinnah (centre) meets Lord Mountbatten and his wife, Edwina, in 1947.

While Mountbatten wrestled with this problem he encouraged Gandhi and Jinnah to issue a joint statement on 15 April 1947, deploring the "recent acts of lawlessness and violence that have brought the utmost disgrace on the fair name of India" and denouncing "for all time the use of force to achieve political ends". Gandhi still believed that he could keep India united through non-violence while Jinnah was prepared to break up India via violent means if necessary.

On 3 June 1947 Mountbatten announced his decision. He proposed to divide India in two, to create the mainly Hindu state of India and the Muslim state of Pakistan, and to allow the state legislatures (parliaments) of Bengal and Punjab to decide for themselves if they wanted to remain united in India or to agree to partition themselves to allow their Muslim-majority areas to join Pakistan. If Bengal decided on partition, the Muslim-majority district of Sylhet in Assam could vote whether to join Muslim Bengal as part of Pakistan or remain in India. Independence Day was brought forward 10 months from June 1948 to 15 August 1947, a little over three months away.

The division of India

The Congress Party met in New Delhi on 15 June to discuss the plan and voted in support in order to avoid further violence and the possibility of civil war. The Muslim League, too, reluctantly agreed. Gandhi, however, disagreed with his own Congress Party and remained opposed to partition. He received many abusive letters from Hindus asking why he supported the Muslims, and from Muslims asking why he continued to obstruct the creation of Pakistan.

Gandhi however believed that 32 years of his life – ever since he had returned from South Africa in 1915 – had "come to an inglorious end" and considered partition "a spiritual tragedy" and a failure of his non-violent leadership. "I deceived myself into the belief that people were wedded to non-violence," Gandhi said, and considered that they had betrayed that for the less important goal of political independence. Gandhi always viewed *swaraj* – home rule – as including freedom from fear and ignorance, not just freedom from Britain or freedom at all costs, and felt that much had been lost in the rush to obtain purely political independence.

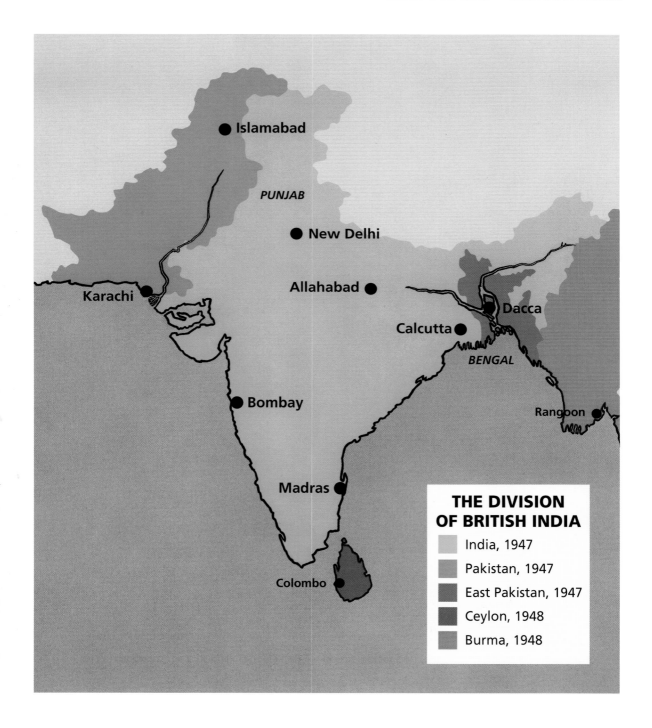

Islamabad

PUNJAB

New Delhi

Allahabad

Karachi

Dacca

Calcutta

BENGAL

Bombay

Rangoon

Madras

Colombo

THE DIVISION OF BRITISH INDIA

- India, 1947
- Pakistan, 1947
- East Pakistan, 1947
- Ceylon, 1948
- Burma, 1948

At midnight on 15 August 1947 – Independence Day – India became independent from Britain and the new Muslim state of Pakistan was carved out of it. The Punjab and Bengal were divided in two, with the Sylhet district of Assam voting to join Pakistani East Bengal. The eastern and western parts of Pakistan were separated by 1300 km of India, out of whose 330 million people, 42 million were Muslim. Most of the 565 native or princely states joined India immediately, with three joining Pakistan. The Hindu ruler of Muslim-dominated Kashmir hesitated to join either state, but an invasion by Muslim tribesmen backed by Pakistan led to a division of the state between the two countries.

Mountbatten stayed on as the first governor-general of India, a position held by Jinnah in Pakistan. Both countries joined the British Commonwealth, an organization of former British colonies such as Canada, Australia, New Zealand and South Africa, which were now independent nations.

◄ *Jubilant crowds break through cordons in the streets of New Delhi to shake hands with Lord and Lady Mountbatten on 15 August 1947, India's first full day of independence.*

The death of Gandhi

The last six months of Gandhi's life were lived in an independent India torn apart by religious strife.

On Independence Day – 15 August 1947 – Gandhi refused to attend the official celebrations in New Delhi. Instead, he travelled to the vast city of Calcutta, in Indian West Bengal. Here a quarter of the population were Muslim, yet they lived in fear for their lives in Hindu-dominated India. The partition of India at independence led to widespread chaos, death and destruction as Muslims fled to safety in Pakistan, and Hindus fled in the other direction to India. About 14 million people became refugees, and at least 500,000 were killed in the inter-communal rioting that accompanied independence.

Gandhi was appalled by this violence, which was especially fierce in Calcutta. He spent Independence Day fasting and praying for peace. Over the next few weeks he held daily prayer meetings, which were attended by thousands of Indians of all religions, and gradually the violence subsided. However, on the night of 31 August, Gandhi was sleeping in the house of a Muslim when a mob attacked the house and broke all the windows. Gandhi was fortunate to escape without serious injury.

Gandhi decided that he must respond to this violence and announced the next day that at 8.15 p.m. he would begin a "fast unto death" in order to bring peace and order to Calcutta. Over the next couple of days, religious and city leaders came to talk to Gandhi. Police officers held a 24-hour sympathy fast while they were on duty, and by 4 September 1947 Calcutta was at peace. Gandhi began to eat again, and for the rest of the year,

▶ *In the last year of his life, Gandhi held regular prayer meetings, at which he prayed in public for peace in India. By now frail, Gandhi often leaned on the shoulders of young women in his entourage.*

Calcutta and both parts of Bengal – Indian West Bengal and Pakistani East Bengal – remained at peace, a remarkable testament to Gandhi's influence and prestige.

▼ *On 22 September 1947, Gandhi visited Muslim refugees at the Purana Qila camp, where 50,000 refugees awaited transport to their new life in Pakistan.*

The force of peace

Lord Mountbatten remarked that in Calcutta Gandhi had achieved more through moral persuasion than "four armed divisions might have achieved by force", but violence continued elsewhere in India. Prime Minister Nehru asked

Gandhi to travel across the country to the partitioned province of Punjab, where the violence was at its worst. Here Hindu and Sikh refugees were fleeing with all their belongings from Pakistani West Punjab in a 91-km column into the Indian East Punjab. Many thousands were losing their lives along the way.

On his way to the Punjab, Gandhi stopped in the capital, New Delhi, where many of the Punjabi refugees had settled in vast camps around the outskirts of the city. It was his 78th birthday, and many people sent flowers and congratulations, but Gandhi asked, "Would it not be more appropriate to send condolences? There is nothing but anguish in my heart. Time was whatever I said the masses followed. Today, mine is a lone voice … I cannot live while hatred and killing mar the atmosphere … I therefore plead with you to give up the present madness."

The final fast

The violence in Delhi persuaded Gandhi to remain in the capital and undertake another "fast unto death" in order to bring peace to the city. He was staying at Birla House, a vast mansion made available for his use, as his preferred lodging in the untouchables quarter of the city was overflowing with refugees. Gandhi began his fast at noon on 13 January 1948. Huge crowds gathered outside, but some were hostile and shouted "Gandhi *morbadad*" (death to Gandhi). Within two days, his health gave way, prompting more than a hundred representatives of various religious and community groups to agree a resolution to maintain peace. Hindu and Muslim leaders signed the agreement, leading Gandhi to end his fast.

For the rest of the month, Gandhi stayed at Birla House, meeting journalists and politicians and holding prayer meetings. On 20 January, a bomb exploded at one of these meetings. It was thrown by a Hindu who had fled the violence in the Punjab and found refuge in a deserted Muslim mosque in Delhi. However, the police had evicted him and the other squatters in order to return the building to its Muslim worshippers. Gandhi bore his attacker no ill will, and instead asked people to pity him.

The death of Gandhi

On the afternoon of Friday 30 January 1948, Gandhi walked into the garden of

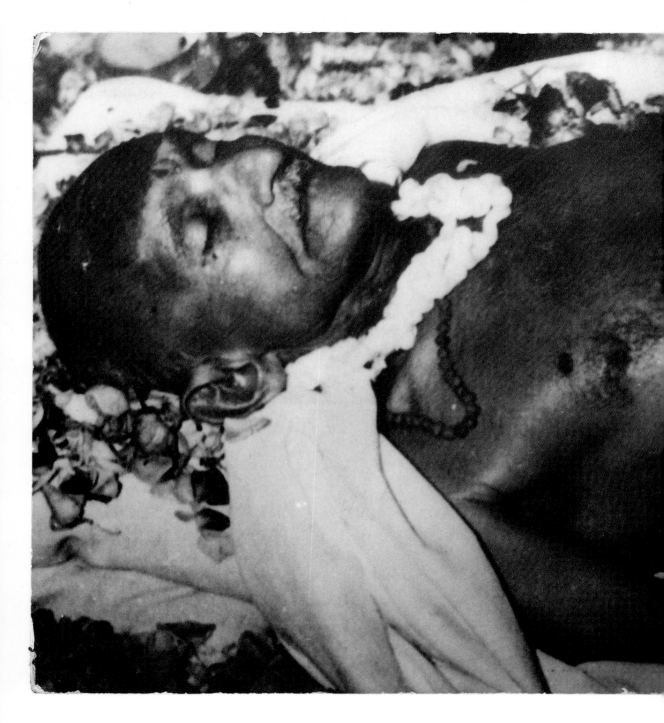

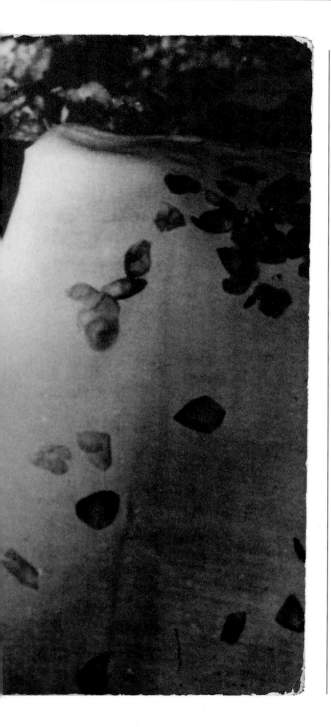

Birla House to conduct his usual evening prayer meeting. Nathuram Godse, who had been involved in the attempted bomb attack on Gandhi ten days before, sat in the front row of the waiting congregation. He bowed to Gandhi – who returned the compliment to Godse and the rest of the congregation – and then shot Gandhi three times. Gandhi fell to the ground; his last words were "Hey Rama" (Oh God).

Gandhi was laid to rest on the roof of Birla House, where the vast crowds could catch a last glimpse of him. Prime Minister Nehru and Gandhi's son, Devadas, soon came to the house, as did thousands of other mourners. News of Gandhi's death was broadcast to the Indian nation by Nehru on All-India Radio. "The light has gone out in our lives and there is darkness everywhere," said Nehru, "and I do not quite know what to tell you and how to say it. Our beloved leader . . . the father of our nation, is no more . . . the light that shone in this country was no ordinary light."

◀ *After his death, Gandhi's body was covered in rose petals and laid on the roof of Birla House so that the vast crowds could catch a last glimpse of him.*

The next morning, a vast funeral procession left on the five-and-a-half-mile journey to the cremation site on the banks of the River Jamuna. A million and a half people marched with the cortege, while another million watched by the side of the road. In a traditional Hindu service, Gandhi was laid on top of a funeral pyre of sandalwood. When his son Ramdas lit the fire at 4.45 p.m., the crowd cried out "Mahatmaji amar ho gae!" (Mahatma has become immortal). As the pyre burned, the entire text of the *Bhagavad Gita* was read out loud. When the fire finally went out, some of Gandhi's ashes were collected and given to friends and dignitaries around the world, while others were scattered in India's many holy rivers. Most were taken by train to be scattered 14 days later at Hinduism's holiest site. The train journey was often interrupted to allow huge crowds of mourners to pay their final respects before the ashes arrived at Allahabad, the holy meeting place of the sacred Ganges and Jamuna rivers and the invisible, heavenly Saraswati river.

▶ *Gandhi's body was escorted by army officers and policemen and carried on a weapons carrier through Delhi.*

The legacy of Gandhi

When Gandhi died in January 1948, he held no elected office in India, did not represent his country in any international organization, and had won no international prize. Yet his contribution to the world was immense.

Gandhi was the first modern politician to promote the use of non-violence to achieve political ends. The 20th century was marked by two world wars, acts of genocide and mass murder, and numerous wars and conflicts around the world, as well as the development of weapons of mass destruction. Yet Gandhi stood out against that violence. He devised a method – satyagraha – of using peaceful protest to achieve peaceful change. "Non-violence is the greatest force at the disposal of mankind. It is mightier than the mightiest weapon of destruction devised by the ingenuity of man," he wrote.

▼ *Like Gandhi, civil rights leader Martin Luther King Jr. believed in a strategy of non-violence to achieve political aims. Here he waves to the crowds at the end of the successful March on Washington civil rights demonstration on 30 August 1963.*

Martin Luther King

That message of non-violent action to achieve peaceful change has been taken up by many people around the world, notably Martin Luther King Jr. and the civil rights movement in the USA. During the 1950s and 1960s, King and his fellow campaigners staged sit-ins in segregated restaurants and other public facilities, boycotted segregated buses, held voter registration marches throughout the southern states, and marched on the national capital of Washington DC in order to draw attention to the inequalities and lack of civil rights for black people in the USA. Their actions were often met by violence from local people and from hostile police forces, but King always met violence with peace.

Like Gandhi, King used many different tactics, such as prayer meetings – he was a Christian minister – marches and sit-ins, to achieve his ends. He visited India during the 1950s, after the death of Gandhi, and saw for himself the results of Gandhi's work. Although King was only 39 when he was assassinated in 1968, he did live to see the enactment of the 1964 Civil Rights Act and the 1965 Voting Rights Act, both of which did much to remove institutional racism and discrimination against black people in the USA. King owed much to Gandhi. He said that, "If humanity is to progress, Gandhi is inescapable. He lived, thought, and acted inspired by a vision of humanity evolving toward a world of peace and harmony. We may ignore Gandhi at our own risk."

The message of non-violence has also been taken up elsewhere in the world, including Northern Ireland, where civil rights marchers crossed the province from Belfast to Derry in January 1969 in order to achieve equality for Roman Catholics who were discriminated against by the majority Protestant population. Peace movements and anti-nuclear and anti-war activists in Europe – notably the women peace campaigners at Greenham Common airbase in England and the anti-nuclear demonstrators in Germany – have all used Gandhi as an example in their campaigns to rid the world of arms and conflict, although few have had the success that Gandhi did.

▶ *Anti-nuclear activists peacefully sit down on a stretch of railway line at Leitstade near Dannenberg on 27 March 2001, as German riot police prepare to clear the track.*

▲ When Indian salt farmers protested in June 1998 against the government decision to allow only iodised salt to be sold, many people remembered the similar campaign by Gandhi against British salt laws in 1930.

Interestingly, Gandhi never won the main international prize for peace, the Nobel Peace Prize, awarded every year since 1901 to a person or organization who has contributed most to the cause of world peace and understanding. Although he was nominated five times between 1937 and 1948, many members of the Nobel Committee felt that he was, at that time, too closely identified with the cause of Indian independence and not enough with the wider cause of world peace to win the prize. In addition, it was considered difficult to award him the prize in 1947 when India and Pakistan were in conflict over Kashmir. More recent winners, such as the Dalai Lama in 1989, have paid tribute to his work.

His effect on India

The main impact of Gandhi's life has been felt in his native India. Here, against all the odds of poverty, illiteracy and underdevelopment, the world's most populated democracy has flourished in a part of the world where few countries are democracies and many have military or repressive governments.

India has also remained secular, despite the growing strength of Hindu militancy.

Hindus, Muslims, Sikhs, Christians and others live together in some sort of peace. Today, Muslims make up about 11 per cent of the total Indian population – around 110 million out of 997 million – which makes India the largest and most successful Muslim democracy in the world. Other large Muslim states, such as Pakistan and Indonesia, have all had long periods of military rule. Gandhi objected to the creation of a Muslim-only Pakistan, as he wanted all the peoples of India to live peacefully together, whatever their faith. Although India is often disfigured by violence, it remains the largest, most successful multi-religious and multi-ethnic country in the world.

Economically, India remains a basically poor country, but its people can feed and clothe themselves. Gandhi's campaigns to revive village life and encourage people to spin and weave their own cloth did much to educate and support India's growing rural population and prepare them for independence from Britain and self-sufficiency.

His effect on individuals

It is very difficult to measure the impact an important and influential person has made after their death, or what their legacy has been to the world. In Gandhi's case, it is almost impossible, because he ran no government and fought no war. But Gandhi did have an enormous impact on individuals. Some, like Martin Luther King, are well known, while most remain unknown. But all of them, and the lives of people around them, were transformed by Gandhi's example, which they tried to copy in their own countries.

In India, the harijans had their lives transformed by Gandhi's intervention, as did many others who heard him speak or read his writings and tried to put his teachings into practice. Across the world, millions of people have tried to change the world peacefully in order to make it a better place in which to live. As long as mankind suffers war, injustice and poverty, Gandhi will be remembered as someone who showed everybody how to challenge those evils without doing evil oneself.

▶ *The image of Mahatma Gandhi in his homespun cotton clothes, as here in London in 1931, is today as familiar to millions as any living politician.*

Glossary

ashram
A religious community practising self-sufficiency and living apart from the rest of the world.

caste system
Ancient Hindu division of society that places people in one of five social castes or classes.

colony
A region or country that is controlled by another country. People who settle in a colony are known as colonists.

Congress
The Indian National Congress, the major political party in India, established in 1885.

constitution
The written document that lays out the fundamental principles of how a country is to be governed.

electorate
The citizens of a country able to vote for their representatives in government.

empire
A large number of different countries conquered and ruled by one government or leader.

fast
To abstain from eating some or all foods; Gandhi used fasting for political ends.

federation
A country where several provinces or states are joined together in a single union.

genocide
The deliberate killing of an entire nationality or ethnic group.

harijans
See untouchables.

hartal

An ancient form of popular protest or strike involving prayers, fasting and processions, popularized by Gandhi in 1919.

Hinduism

The ancient religion of India; its followers are called Hindus.

indentured labourer

A person who is tied into a fixed-term contract. In this book, Indians worked on five-year contracts on private farms or in mines in southern Africa in return for free board and lodgings, a guaranteed wage and free passage home for themselves and their families at the end of the period agreed in the contract. For a fee, an Indian could buy his way out of the contract.

Islam

The religion founded by the prophet Mohammad in Arabia in the 7th century; its followers are called Muslims.

khadi

Homespun cloth.

Mahatma

Title given to Gandhi by Rabindranath Tagore; it means "great soul".

monopoly

Exclusive control of the production and or supply of particular goods or services.

nationalist

A person who loves his or her own country and supports, and sometimes fights, for it.

Pakistan

The Muslim state carved out of east and west India when it became independent in 1947. The name Pakistan means "land of the pure" from the Urdu words *pak*, which means pure, and *stan*, which means land.

partition

Dividing a country into two or more parts.

pilgrimage

A journey to a sacred place or one for a religious purpose, such as peace.

prime minister

The political leader of a country with a parliamentary democracy.

prince

Ruler of an Indian state under British rule; many of the princes were known as maharajahs.

Raj

The period of British rule in India.

republic

A country with no monarchy, where the people elect their head of state either directly at the ballot box or through their representatives in parliament.

round-table conference

A meeting, on equal terms, of opposing political groups to have discussions.

satyagraha

Literally truth-force or love-force; the use of non-violent civil resistance to achieve political or economic change.

swaraj

Home rule, or self-rule, for India.

swardeshi

The use of Indian home-grown, spun, and manufactured goods only.

trading post

A settlement established by foreigners for the purposes of trade and commerce with the local people.

untouchables

The lowest of the five castes or classes in the Hindu religion; Gandhi called them harijans, "children of god".

vegetarian

Someone who does not eat meat or fish.

viceroy

The British governor of India, representing the British monarch and government in the country.

Timeline

1869 2 October Born in Porbandar, India.

1875 Starts school in Porbandar.

1882 Marries Kasturbai.

1885 Indian National Congress set up in Bombay; Death of Karamchand Gandhi, Mohandas' father.

1887 Birth of first son Harilal; Manilal is born in 1892, Ramdas in 1897, Devadas in 1900.

1888–91 Studies law in London and qualifies as a barrister.

1893 Starts a new life in South Africa.

1903 Opens law practice in Johannesburg in the Transvaal.

1904 Creates his first ashram, the Phoenix Settlement, outside Durban.

1906 Launches first satyagraha campaign in South Africa.

1908 Sentenced to first period in jail, for disobeying the Asian Registration Act.

1910 Establishes Tolstoy Farm outside Johannesburg.

1913 Fasts for first time, to protest against the treatment of Indians in South Africa.

1914 Wins substantial agreement on Indian rights; leaves South Africa and returns to India.

1915 Establishes Satyagraha Ashram outside Ahmedabad.

1919 Hartal against the Rowlatt Bills leads to mass violence and the Amritsar Massacre.

1920 Becomes President of the All-India Home Rule League.

1922–24 Imprisoned for inciting civil unrest.

1926 Year of silence.

1928 Simon Commission visits India to look at new constitution; Gandhi leads Bardoli tax strike in protest.

1930 Leads Salt March.

1931 Visits London for round-table talks on the future government of India.

1932 "Fast unto death" leads to victory for the untouchables.

1933 Establishes Sevagram Ashram in Wardha.

1934 Becomes patron of All-India Village Industries Association; Muhammad Ali Jinnah starts to campaign for the partition of India.

1939 World War Two breaks out in Europe.

1940 Gandhi launches a person-by-person satyagraha against British rule.

1942 Cripps' mission to India; Congress launches "Quit India" campaign; Gandhi imprisoned.

1944 Death of Kasturbai; Gandhi released from prison; talks with Jinnah prove unsuccessful.

1945 Labour government in Britain agrees to independence for India.

1946 British mission to India proposes a united, federal state; Nehru becomes Prime Minister; Direct Action Day leads to massive inter-communal violence across India; Gandhi travels to Bengal to spread message of peace.

1947 India and Pakistan become independent; Gandhi visits Calcutta and then New Delhi to keep the peace; Lord Mountbatten arrives in India as the last viceroy and proposes the partition of India.

1948 30 January Gandhi assassinated in New Delhi

Further reading

Blais, Genevieve, *Gandhi: A Beginner's Guide,* London: Hodder & Stoughton, 2000

Clement, Catherine, *Gandhi, Father of a Nation,* London: Thames & Hudson, 1996

Fischer, Louis, *The Life of Mahatma Gandhi,* London: HarperCollins, 1951

Fischer, Louis (ed.), *The Essential Gandhi: An Anthology of his Writings on His Life, Work and Ideas,* New York: Vintage Books, 1962

Mukherjee, Rudrangshu (ed.), *The Penguin Gandhi Reader,* New York: Penguin Books, 1993

Rühe, Peter, *Gandhi,* London: Phaidon Press, 2001

Watson, Francis *India, A Concise History,* London: Thames & Hudson, 1979

Throughout his life, Gandhi wrote a stream of letters, newspaper articles, books and pamphlets, as well as a brief autobiography and other writings. His most important work was *Hind Swaraj* or Indian Home Rule, which he wrote in South Africa in 1909. In it, he summed up his philosophy:

"Real home rule is self rule or self-control.

"The way to it is passive resistance: that is soul-force or love-force.

"In order to exert this force, swadeshi in every sense is necessary.

"What we want to do should be done, not because we object to the English or because we want to retaliate but because it is our duty to do so. Thus, supposing the English remove the salt tax, restore our money, give the highest posts to Indians, withdraw the English troops, we shall certainly not use their machine-made goods, nor use the English language, nor many of their industries. It is worth noting that these things are, in their nature, harmful; hence we do not want them. I bear no enmity towards the English but I do towards their civilization."

Index

Page numbers in italics are pictures or maps.